You Can Be Mortgage Free

How To Pay Off Your Mortgage Early

BY: Matthew E Hamm

Copyright © 2019 by Matthew E Hamm

All rights reserved. No part of this book may be reproduced in any form on or by an electronic or mechanical means, including information storage and retrieval systems, without permission in writing from the publisher, except by a reviewer who may quote brief passages in a review.

The advice and strategies found within may not be suitable for every situation. This work is sold with the understanding that neither the author nor the publisher are held responsible for the results accrued from the advice in this book.

REinvestWise.com

Contents

Introduction

Where To Start

Make A Budget

Get A Good Mortgage

Find The Right House

Make Extra Payments

You CAN Be Mortgage Free

Introduction

Have you ever wondered what it would be like living mortgage free? I had this dream for as long as I can remember. I am lucky enough to be able to say that I have achieved this goal.

I will not lie to you and say that it was easy or there is a secret to paying your house off fast. I am sure you have seen "click bait" ads that says something like "One Thing Your Mortgage Company Doesn't Want You to Know", let's be honest, there are no tricks.

In this book I will share with you how I paid my mortgage off in under five years and I will guide you in creating a plan to pay your home off fast too, but first I want to tell you who I am.

Who is Matt Hamm?

I am a Realtor with Nova Star Real Estate. I currently manage the Massillon Ohio branch of the company. I work with Buyers, Sellers and Investors. I serve clients in the Residential and Commercial markets.

Before I obtained my real estate salesperson license, I was a home Inspector. I got my education for home inspection and real estate from Hondros College. This is a great school choice for the real estate industry because of their high success rate.

I was a home inspector for about two years before I received my real estate salesperson license. I continued to inspect houses for a couple years after this but then I decided to hang up the inspector career to focus more on real estate sales and investing.

I started out investing in real estate without any guidance or education in this specific area. I looked at a few properties and finally bought one. Again, I had no guidance and the purchase wasn't horrible, but it wasn't what I planned. I highly recommend getting some training, guidance or at least doing some research when you set out to do anything, especially investing.

If you are interested in real estate investing and you would like more information, check out my book **"Anyone Can Invest In Real Estate"**.

Looking back on my own experiences I realized how much easier things could have been if I had someone to help me and guide me. This has allowed me to realize the need for guidance and education in the area of paying off a mortgage early.

This book, **"You Can Be Mortgage Free"**, is the result of this need. I hope that you find it helpful and I know it will help you become **Mortgage Free.**

Chapter One

Where To Start

Everyone reading this will be in all different stages of their life. Some might be looking to buy a home for the first time, some might be a few years into their mortgage and some might be getting closer to the end of their mortgage.

In realizing this I determined to write this book to be helpful to all readers no matter what stage of your mortgage you are in.

My goal is for this book to be helpful to all readers and allow everyone of you to be mortgage free and find financial freedom.

The First Step

The very first thing that must happen before you can pay off your mortgage early is... **You must be determined!**

This will be the first Mountain you will need to climb!

You must retrain your mind. You must always be thinking I am going to pay my mortgage off early. Whether you are a good saver, or you like to spend money as fast as you get it, you will be adjusting your thinking process to always putting money towards your goal of paying your mortgage off.

I am one who hates loans and mortgages. My desire when I was a child and young teenager was to buy everything in cash. I eventually found out this was not always possible.

I bought my first car with cash and it wasn't until I was almost thirty years old until I bought a car with a loan. As much as I wanted to buy a home with cash it was just not possible, so I got a mortgage to purchase a home.

When my wife and I bought our house, we said we would pay it off in five years. Most people thought we were crazy and maybe we were, but we did it in just under five years.

We obtained a thirty-year mortgage and paid it off in under five years and anyone can do it too! There is nothing special or magical about us. We were only making around $40,000 a year together when we bought our home and the most, we ever made together was $65,000 a year.

I'm telling you all of this to say **Anyone can pay off their mortgage early!** Anyone can do it!

It will be tough, but it can be done. You must want to do it. For me, every time I had to spend money I thought, "I could be putting this money towards my mortgage". You will become this way too.

Paying your mortgage off earlier is just like any other goal you might have. You must be all in and you must work at it to make it happen. It all starts with your mindset.

This brings us to...

The Second Step

By now you have your mind trained to always be thinking "I have to pay my mortgage off early". Now you must make it happen.

It will get hard and you will want to give up, but you need to keep at it. You need to be prepared to handle financial issues and not allow yourself to fall behind.

You need to work hard to get ahead and start building a savings account and paying down debt.

The key to the whole process of paying off your mortgage is to put every extra dollar towards your debt. Every dollar you make has the potential to be one less dollar of debt you owe.

You will need to make tough decisions and stick to them. You will need to alter your lifestyle to live more conservatively financially and be happy. It will be a fine line to walk trying to be frugal and enjoy life.

You can do both, I did. I was able to enjoy my life with my family and save money and pay down my mortgage.

Now that you know where it all starts, that is, within yourself. Your own willpower and your mindset need to be determined to pay off your mortgage. You now understand that paying an extra dollar towards your mortgage is more important then getting that candy bar.

In the remainder of this book we will go over the steps involved in the process of paying off your mortgage early, so you can be **Mortgage Free!**

Chapter Two

Make A Budget

This is the second mountain you need to climb.

When someone says "make a budget" you probably get a bad feeling come over you, like a sour taste in your mouth. I know for me to sit down and write a budget is hard to do. It takes time and it takes work just to write it let alone trying to follow it.

First, we are going to focus on writing a budget. We will get to following a budget later.

Writing A Budget

You are going to need to actually schedule some time to do this. I understand that it's hard to find time in our busy, nonstop lives today, but it needs to be done.

Schedule Time to Make A Budget: Write It Down

You can't just say that you are going to do it tonight. I am wanting you to really put in on your schedule. I schedule everything on my calendar on my phone. It's the easiest way for me to write it down and to access it anywhere I am at.

Before I had a smart phone my wife and I would actually write everything down on the calendar hanging on the wall. We still have a calendar on the wall and we do write some things down like vacations and the kids doctor appointments but for the most part I put everything in my phone calendar. Even the items we write on the wall calendar still go into my phone.

It does not matter how you want to handle your schedule, but for this task, it needs written down and planned for.

Plan for Your Budgeting Session

Making a budget is not something you can just sit down and do. I know in the past when I tried to make a budget I would sit down and start trying to think of every bill I pay, and the amounts owed. Let me tell you, this is impossible. There might be one or two people out there that can do this but I'm guessing the vast majority of people are like me and cannot remember every dollar paid to every bill.

You will need to gather every bill you pay, but not just your monthly bills but also your quarterly, six month and yearly bills as well.

I like to be on a budget for as many bills as I can. It gives me an exact amount that I will pay consistently though out the entire year.

HINT: I also like to put my bills on auto pay through my credit card so that I can get tons of rewards points just by paying my bills that I would be paying anyways. This method is not good for everyone though. I pay off my full balance for my credit card every single month, if you are not good at doing this, I would advise you to continue paying your bills by check.

HINT: doing the above method of auto paying your bills with a credit card and then paying the credit card balance down to zero every month will also help boost your credit score. This may take time, so be consistent and patient.

Once you have made for certain that you have every single bill that you pay for the entire year put it all in one safe place until the scheduled time to make your budget.

Doing this a few days ahead of time allows you to be confident that you have every bill and that you didn't forget any.

Sit Down and Write Your Budget

Make sure you don't miss your appointment to make your budget. This is extremely important, and you need to treat it that way.

Turn off all distractions like the TV and even your PHONE, yes turn off your PHONE. Grab a real calculator so you can't use the excuse of having to use the calculator on your phone and then somehow Facebook turns on or YouTube and you end up distracting yourself for hours. I know first hand how much time is wasted on our smart phones.

You need to make sure you have everything that you will need with you, so you don't have to get up. Grab extra pens or pencils, paper and even a glass of water if you would like. Just make sure everything you need is there.

This includes EVERYONE you need as well. If you have a spouse, they need to help make the budget with you. You will need to be a team on this and both of you need to be all in.

When I make a budget, I like to use one page for all my monthly bills and a separate page for my non-monthly bills.

On the Next page you will find a blank copy of my monthly budget form. You can also download them from my website **REinvestWise.com/Resources** in the Home Owners Section.

You will notice that there is a spot for non-monthly expenses that you will need to write the total from the second page in this spot. We will go over this after we go over the first page of the budget.

Income	Week 1	Week 2	Week 3	Week 4	Week 5
Wages - A					
Wages - B					
Rent(s)					
Royalties/Interests					
Miscellaneous					
				TOTAL:	_____

EXPENSE	Due Date	PAID	Budget	Actual	Difference +/-
Mortgage - First					
Mortgage - Second					
Car Loan - A					
Car Loan - B					
Student Loan - A					
Student Loan - B					
Personal Loan					
Credit Card - A					
Credit Card - B					
Electric					
Water					
Gas					
Sewer					
Cable/Internet					
Phone					
Health Insurance					
Car Insurance					
Gasoline					
Groceries/Food					
MISC: _____					
MISC: _____					
MISC: _____					
NON-Monthly					
Savings					
			TOTAL:	_____	

Total Income	_____
Total Expenses	_____
Difference +/-	_____

REinvestWise.com

Now let's take a closer look at the budget and go over each column and section to make sure you fully understand the whole budget.

The top section is for your monthly income. You will want to add all of your earned and unearned income; your Wages, Rental Property income, Royalties and earned Interest. After you write it all down you will want to total it at the end of the month and then transfer that total to the bottom of the budget on the **Total Income** line.

In the second section you will find the location for your monthly expenses. You will need to write down all of your bills' names on the first column if not already on the list.

The second column you will have a Due Date for each bill. This is extremely important. It may seem simple but paying your bills on time every month will save you thousands of dollars in your life on late fees and added interest due to higher interest rates on loans.

The third column is for you to mark when you actually PAID the bill. Just simply put an X in the box when the bill was paid, alternatively you could write the date the bill was paid in the box. The second option is in my opinion a better option. If you ever have an issue to come up it will make things go much easier for you if you have a date written down when the bill was paid.

The fourth column is for you to write in an estimated budgeted amount for each bill. The idea is to be as accurate as you can on the budgeted amount and this will become easier as the months go by.

The fifth column is for you to write in the actual amount for the bill. With your common bill, like electric or water, you will write the actual amount on this line as soon as you get the bill. Other items like gasoline and groceries you will need to wait until the end of the month to know the actual amount spent and write it in.

With these items you will want to keep a running total throughout the month, so you will know if you are getting close to your budgeted amount.

The last column is where you will write the difference in the budgeted amount and the actual amount spent. This is very important. This will allow you to see where your overages are, and it will allow you to quickly determine what areas you need to work on.

When we get to the part of paying down your mortgage you will see the necessity of trying to spend as little as possible on your budget to allow you to put more money towards paying off your mortgage quickly.

I also want to point out that I put "Groceries and Food" (which is eating out) in the same category. On some budgets I have seen, they will separate these two items. If you want to or feel the need to you can separate them and put one of these items on a MISC line.

It may be easier for you to see where your money is going by doing this.

You may also see that I left a spot for "Savings". It is extremely important to budget a specific amount toward savings every single month. It is tempting to say that you will just put what's left into savings at the end of the month, but I find that there tends to be very little or nothing left at the end of the month.

It becomes much easier to put money into savings when you write it into your budget. I also suggest putting your specified amount into your savings toward the beginning of the month. I like to put the "Due Date" within the first two weeks of the month. This will give you a much higher chance of getting the correct amount into savings and not spending it elsewhere.

You may see some items on the budget that you pay directly out of your paycheck. You can simply leave these items off your budget as long as you use your take home amount of your paycheck in the income section of the budget.

If you want to put these on your budget to see exactly where all of your money is going then you will need to make sure you add the amount back into your paycheck for your income.

As a self-employed Realtor and Real Estate Investor I pay everything out of pocket. Therefore, I have put these items on my budget.

Some of my bills that are on the budget I pay as a "Non-monthly" bill. For example, I pay my car insurance once every six months because of the discount I receive by doing so. You will see my Non-Monthly Budget on the next page.

NON-Monthly Budget

EXPENSE	Due Date	PAID	Budget	Actual	Monthly
Sewer					
Property Tax					
Home Insurance					
Health Insurance					
Car Insurance					
MISC: _____					
MISC: _____					
MISC: _____					
MISC: _____					
				TOTAL:	_____

NOTE: Add the total amount to the Budget on the NON-Monthly line.

You can easily make your own budget, or you can download mine for free from my website **REinvestWise.com/Resources** in the Homeowner section.

You may have different bills than I do in this area. I did not put all my non-monthly bills on there because they will not apply to many people. I am a Realtor and I have quite a few different "DUES" that I owe every six months. All these bills would go on the non-monthly budget page.

The last column is different on the non-monthly budget page. It is labeled "MONTHLY". This is for you to write in the amount you will need to put into savings or a separate account for you to pay the non-monthly bills when they are due.

To figure out what the monthly amount would be you just divide the billed amount by how many months it covers.

For Example, if you pay $300 for car insurance every six months, you would simply divide $300 by six months and you would get a monthly total of $50. So, you would write $50 on the Monthly line for Car Insurance and each month you will need to set aside $50 for your car insurance.

The timing gets a little tricky with this non-monthly budget. Depending on when you start using this budget you may need to supplement your account for these non-monthly bills. If you start you budget in May and your six-month car insurance bill is due in June, then you would not have enough time to save up the correct amount of money before the bill is due.

It would be best to figure out the difference and put that amount into the account right from the beginning. Using our same car insurance example, you will owe $300 for car insurance in June. You started your budget in May. You will only make one "Payment" into your separate account for your non-monthly bills. This will give your $50 towards the $300 bill. You will need to make up the $250 difference and it is best to do this in the beginning when you first start the budget.

If your personal finances do not allow you to put all this money in this separate account all at once, then you should divide it up by the number of months left before the bill. In our example there was only one month left but if we had three months to make up the difference it would only be an additional $50 per month. You would only need to put in $50 a month on top of the $50 a month you are already putting in the account for the car insurance.

Here is how I figured this out:

$50 per month budgeted for car insurance

X 3 months of payments

$150 put into an account for non-monthly bills

$300 car insurance bill due

- $150 already put into the non-monthly account

$150 difference that you will need to make up

$150 deficit

÷ 3 months to make up the difference

$50 per month of additional savings

You will need to do this for all your non-monthly bills to make sure you have enough money put aside for each bill when it is due. Once you make one payment for each bill you can go to the budgeted amount for each bill and you will not have to put any additional money into this account.

The bills will more then likely be due in different months, so this mean you will not stop making the additional payments all at once. This is a good thing though because this means you will not have to make huge extra payments into this separate account for very long, maybe only a month or two.

I want to point out that the non-monthly bill savings account should be separate from your tradition savings account. You want this money to be separate. My bank allows me to have as many savings accounts as I want with no additional charge, so I just had them make me a separate savings account for these non-monthly bills.

Your traditional savings account should be for EMERGENCIES only, not your monthly or non-monthly bills. I could go over the many reasons for this, but this is not a personal finance book, my goal is to set you up to successfully pay off your mortgage early.

The goal of your budget is to show you where your money is going and to help you free up more money to put towards your mortgage.

The "Actual" amount paid for your bills, including your savings and non-monthly, at the end of the month needs to be less then your income.

You will see on the bottom of the first page of the budget there is a place to figure out the difference of your total monthly income from your total monthly expenses. You need to have a positive difference here. The bigger the difference the faster you can pay off your mortgage.

Your secondary goal should be to have a total "Actual" amount less than your total "Budgeted". This is where you find out how much self-control and determination you have. You will need to cut out things that are wasting your money. If you eat out at a restaurant six days a week and your "Actual" amount is $100 above your "Budgeted" amount, then you should consider cutting out one or two of the days you eat out.

There may be other areas you can work on too, I just picked this one to use as an example since it is one that I personally struggle with. Trying to find $100 a month to cut out of your expenses is actually easier then you might think. There are hundreds of ways to save money each month, like using coupons, eating at home versus eating out, carpool, paying bills online (save a stamp), cutting out extras like candy bars or $5 coffees every day and so many more!

I know some of you just read the coffee comment and thought I was crazy. I am not crazy. I am just suggesting that you make your coffee at home and save $3 or $4 a day. If you go to a "coffee shop" (we all know which ones I am talking about) everyday and buy a drink, it adds up. One report I recently read said the average American spends $3 a day on a coffee drink, that's $1,095 a year or just over $90 a month.

This same philosophy works for any "treat" that we waste our money on. It may be food related or maybe its going to the movies or buying video games. I am not suggesting you cut everything out and live like a prisoner but the more you cut out the faster you can pay off your mortgage.

The strategy I used to pay my mortgage off in under five years works. Using a budget like this will allow you to allocate as much money as possible towards paying down your mortgage quickly. The idea is to use all of the money at the bottom of the budget, the positive difference and put it ALL towards your mortgage payments.

Once you start doing it and seeing your mortgage go down you will get addicted. You will get excited about saving money on the budget and paying it towards your mortgage.

Following a budget can get tough especially when unexpected things come up. It can be done, and you must stay focused and keep moving forward. You can do it, I know you can!

Chapter Three

Get A Good Mortgage

Whether you are getting ready to buy a home or you have been in your home for ten years you need to make sure you have the best mortgage you can get.

What is a good mortgage?

This may not be something that you have considered before. When you bought your home or went to find out if you could get preapproved for a home loan you may have only been concerned about "IF" you could get approved and "HOW MUCH" you could get approved for.

There is more to consider then those two issues. The issues, if you can get approved and how much you can get approved for, are both very important but there is more to home loans then just those two issues.

I want to go over the different types of home loans available and the benefits of them. You may already have the best loan available to you, and if you do that is great, but if not, this information will help you decide what option you should go with.

I will go over both purchase and refinance loans. There will be a few options for both scenarios.

Purchase Loans

These loans are exactly what you think they are, to purchase a home. Most people will have more than one option available, so I will go over the "Pros" and "Cons" of each type of purchase loan. I will go over the most used loan options.

FHA Loan

This is a very common loan product. FHA stands for "Federal Housing Administration". What this means is the federal government insures the loan, they do not give you the loan. A lender will give the loan to you. Almost all lenders and banks offer FHA loans.

Pros:

- Lower Qualifying Credit Score then other options. Some lenders offer 580 but most will require 620
- Lower Down Payment then other options. 3.5%

Cons:

- You are required to carry Mortgage Insurance.
- FHA has higher standards for property condition. (This could be looked at as a positive, but most buyers see it as a negative because they could lose the property that they wanted due to required repairs)

VA Loan

This is also a federal government insured loan product. It has some things in common with FHA. The Eligibility for VA loans is exclusive to Active Duty Service Members and Veterans.

They extend this to the National Guard and the Reserves. There are service time limits (minimums) on all the types of service to be qualified.

Pros:

- 0% Down Payment
- No Mortgage Insurance

Cons:

- Eligibility requirements
- VA has the Highest standards for property condition. (This could be looked at as a positive, but most buyers see it as a negative because they could lose the property that they wanted due to required repairs)

USDA Loan

Again, this is a government loan product. This one has a different set of requirements. The home must be located in an approved rural area and the buyer will have income limitations.

You can find if the location you are looking in is an approved location by checking out the USDA website and typing in an address that you are interested in.

Most lenders and Realtors will be able to tell you if the area you are interested in is an USDA approved area. The benefits make this loan worth checking into to see if you are eligible.

Pros:

- 0% Down Payment
- No limit on seller Contributions (seller paid Closing Cost)

Cons:

- Location Restrictions
- Income Limits

Conventional Loan

This is one of the more popular choices. This is not a government loan product so there are less restrictions involved. Less government and less restrictions are a good thing, right?

Conventional loans are pretty much straight forward, and they are a good option. Going with a conventional loan will require more money upfront for the down payment.

If you have been able to save up enough money to be able to go with a conventional loan, then you have done a great job already! You also have set yourself up to save quite a bit of money on interest by starting with a lower principal amount.

Pros:

- Less restrictions on property condition
- No Mortgage Insurance

Cons:

- Higher Down Payment Requirements
- Higher Income Requirements

Refinance Loans

These loans are for people that already have a home and a mortgage on the home.

There are a few reasons someone should consider refinancing their home but the main thing we are interested in here is the interest rate. This is because the interest rate is one thing that impacts your ability to pay off your mortgage quickly and it also affects how much money you lose to your mortgage company.

The lower your interest rate the more money you can put on your mortgage and pay your mortgage off fast.

There are a few refinance loan product options available, but we are only going to talk about Fixed Rate and Adjustable Rate Loans.

There are cash out options available, but this goes against our plan to pay off your mortgage quickly by adding more debt to your loan. We don't want to do that, this would be counterproductive.

I want to point out that you may not need to refinance your home loan. It only makes sense to do this if you currently have a higher interest rate then what is being offered, but It doesn't hurt to find out what you are being offered.

Fixed Rate Refinance Mortgage

A fixed rate loan is exactly what it sounds like. The interest rate is fixed or stays the same the entire length of the loan.

It is best to get a fixed rate loan when the interest rates are low. When interest rates go up you may want to consider other options or even keeping your current mortgage. If current interest rates are lower, then the rate on your current mortgage then you should consider refinancing with a fixed rate mortgage. If current interest rates are higher then the rate on your current mortgage, then you should not consider a fixed rate mortgage, but you should look at other option such as an Adjustable Rate Mortgage. We will get to that later.

Benefits of a Fixed Rate Mortgage

There are many benefits of refinancing to a fixed rate mortgage. We will go over a few of the biggest benefits.

Stability

This is by far my favorite attribute of a fixed rate mortgage. Your principal and interest payments will always be the same for the entire loan. If you have your taxes and insurance escrowed by your lender and added to the loan, then there is a possibility of that part of the loan payment fluctuating. If your property taxes go up, then the escrow portion of your loan payments will go up.

For the most part you can predict what your payments will be for the length of the loan. This is a great benefit! Having this stability will greatly improve your ability to pay off your mortgage quickly.

You will be able to structure your budget around your mortgage payments and you will be able to predict the extra amount of money you can put towards your mortgage each month.

Simple

Fixed rate mortgages are very simple. What you see is what you get. You won't have to worry about what the real estate market is doing or what the federal government decides to do with interest rates.

You will not have to restructure your budget every time the interest rates change. Interest rates can go up four times a year, but you will not have to worry about that. Your loan stays the same.

It could be possible for the interest rates to go down before the end of your loan or before you pay it off. If this does happen you can just investigate your options of refinancing again, but this probably will not be necessary since you will be paying off your mortgage early.

Disadvantages of a Fixed Rate Mortgage

Interest Rates

Fixed rate mortgages are only good if the current interest rates are lower then the interest rate on your current mortgage. This means if interest rates are up then a fixed rate refinance mortgage may not be a good option for you at this time.

Interest rates change over time and if you go with a fixed rate mortgage you may be stuck paying a higher rate then the current market rate.

Interest rates for fixed rate mortgages are typically higher then an adjustable rate mortgage. When you make your first year or two of payments on your fixed rate mortgage it may be higher then you would have had with an adjustable rate mortgage.

Eligibility

Fixed rate mortgages have higher qualification then other loan options. Not everyone will be able to qualify for a fixed rate mortgage. In some cases, you may qualify for an adjustable rate mortgage but not a fixed rate mortgage.

Debt to income ratio is one of the areas that are stricter with fixed rate mortgages. This is more relaxed with an adjustable rate mortgage.

If you are qualified for a fixed rate mortgage, then this might be your best option.

Adjustable Rate Refinance Mortgage

Adjustable Rate Mortgages, also known as ARM, can be good or bad. You will be at the mercy of the interest rates and housing market. If the interest rates go up, then your rate will go up and you will have to pay more interest on your monthly mortgage payment.

You may be thinking, "If interest rates go down then my mortgage payment will go down too". I hate to say this but that is not necessarily true. You will have to look at your loan documents or ask your loan officer to know for sure but most ARM are written up to not go down but stay the same. If it does go down it won't be much.

Don't worry though, there are some benefits of getting an adjustable rate mortgage and I will go over them with you.

Benefits of Adjustable Rate Mortgages

Easier to Qualify

As I mentioned before, it may be easier to qualify for an adjustable rate mortgage then a fixed rate mortgage. If you don't qualify for that fixed rate mortgage, then try asking your loan officer to check into getting you approved for an adjustable rate mortgage.

Lenders will have different rules and requirements that are specific to their company, especially the smaller independently owned companies. I have saved a few real estate transactions by having the buyer qualify for an adjustable rate mortgage after getting denied the fixed rate mortgage.

Lower Initial Payments

This is one of the best aspects of an adjustable rate mortgage. You will usually but not always get a lower interest rate in the beginning of the loan which will cause your mortgage payments to be lower.

This will also allow you to qualify for a slightly higher priced home. If you find a home that you are in love with, your Dream Home, but it is a few thousand out of your range, then you may be able to still reach that purchase price with an ARM loan. This is because your monthly payments will be slightly lower due to the lower interest.

Faster Pay Off

This is going off the fact that you may get lower payments in the beginning which will allow you to put more money towards the mortgage and pay it off faster.

You will have to be disciplined with your money. You may have good intentions at first but if you have an extra $75 a month you might get tempted to spend it elsewhere. You must put that extra money right back onto the loan.

Disadvantages of Adjustable Rate Mortgages

Unstable Monthly Payments

Your monthly payment can and probably will go up at some point of your adjustable rate mortgage. You really need to do your homework here. Every mortgage company is different and will have different offers for the Adjustable Rate Mortgages.

The longer the initial rate is locked in the better. I often see one to two years for the initial locked rate period. I have heard of some only being a few months, so you will want to know what the initial rate period is before you agree to the mortgage.

You will also want to know how often the rate can change. Traditionally this will be about four times a year, or in other words, quarterly. There are some adjustable rate mortgages that can have rate changes monthly. I would never suggest going with a loan that can increase the rate every month. You can get into trouble quickly and it will be hard to recover from these kinds of rate changes.

Keep in mind that every time your rate goes up you have a lower chance of paying off your mortgage quickly. The more money you pay in interest the less money you can put toward the principal balance.

Interest Rates Are Increasing

Interest rates are current on the low side even though they have been on the rise for a while now. The rates are going to continue to rise. Ten to twenty years ago rates were over ten percent, so we have a long way t go before we reach that point again.

Unless another housing market crash happens, we will not see rates go down for quite a while. You can count on small increases until we get back up to the rates we had before the crash.

May Have to Refinance Again in The Future

If rates keep going up, you could have to refinance again in the future just to be able to keep your payments from rising to high.

In a worst-case scenario, you could end up hitting the max rate increase of six percent. This means if your introduction interest rate is five percent you could end up hitting eleven percent by the end of the term.

Getting a fixed rate mortgage looks much better now doesn't it? Adjustable Rate Mortgages are not all bad, like I mentioned in the Benefits section of this chapter there are reasons to go with an ARM.

Additional Thoughts on Mortgages

Payoff Date

The most important thing you need to keep in mind is, what is your realistic early payoff date for your mortgage? If you can pay your mortgage off in under five years, like I did, then an adjustable rate mortgage may be a good option. You can have lower payments in the beginning, and you would be able to put more money on the principal to pay the loan down faster. If it will take you twenty years to pay off your mortgage (which is still good, its ten years early and thousands saved in interest payments) you may not want to go with an adjustable rate mortgage, a fixed rate mortgage may be better in the long run.

Closing Costs

Another thing to keep in mind is the closing cost involved in getting a mortgage. Some mortgages do offer no closing costs, but you will have to qualify for those loans. If you don't qualify for a "no closing cost" loan you will want to know up front exactly what it will cost you to get the loan.

All mortgage companies are different, and they have different closing costs as far as how much they charge for each fee. The lender fees are the biggest expense for home buyers, these fees can go over five thousand dollars on a purchase loan.

Wrapping Closing Costs into the Loan

I never suggest doing this if it is at all possible to avoid. There may be a time or two that I have said this was an ok option, but as a general rule I say no to this option.

The reason I say no to wrapping your closing cost into the loan is because you are actually going to pay interest on your closing cost. You will also be paying on these costs for a few years as well. This is because in the first year of a mortgage you usually only pay about one percent of the principal balance.

Example:

$200,000	Loan Balance
$2,950	Principal Paid in Year One
$9,930	Interest Paid in Year One

In the example above the principal balance paid in the first year is only about 1.4%. If you owed $4,000 in lender fees and added this cost into your loan after one year you would still owe $1,050 for your closing costs.

Worst yet, you still haven't put a penny towards the actual price of the home that you financed. You basically wasted one whole year and you put a whole bunch of money into your lenders pocket.

Seller Paid Closing Costs

This can go either way. You may be able to get a good deal on the home and still get the seller to pay some of the closing costs for you.

In a sellers' market you will probably have to pay more for the home to get the seller to pay some of the closing costs for you.

This ends up being about the same as wrapping the closing costs into the loan, you are basically adding the costs into the loan by paying more for the home. The seller usually doesn't care either way, they care about their bottom line. You can pay $5,000 more for the home and they will give you the $5,000 back in closing costs, but like I said this is just adding your costs into the loan balance and you will be paying interest on it now.

In a buyers' market you can get a great deal on a home and also get the seller to pay for some of your closing costs without having to pay more for the home.

There are many home buyers that will need seller paid closing cost to be able to purchase the home. This is fine, it happens all the time. A buyer may also need to have some of the closing costs wrapped into the loan. If this is the only way to get the deal done, then it will be ok.

If you have time to save up a little more money and pay for more of the closing costs yourself that would be helpful. You will pay less interest on the loan this way.

Sometimes you won't be able to take the time to save up the money and that is ok. If you must move quickly you may not be able to save up enough money for all of the closing costs, but the more you save that faster you can pay off your mortgage.

Prepayment Penalty

No matter what loan product you go with you absolutely need to make sure there is no prepayment penalty or early payoff penalty.

You need to ask this upfront, before you get the loan. It should be one of the first questions you ask your loan officer when you meet them or talk to him or her on the phone.

Some loans have a prepayment penalty attached to the loan and it will be a percentage of the loan value. These can be as high as 3% maybe even higher with certain lenders. On a $250,000 mortgage that would be $7,500. That is quite a bit of money isn't it. Make sure you won't have to pay a prepayment penalty when paying off your home early.

Chapter Four

Find the Right House

This chapter will be focused more towards someone that has not yet bought their home. If you already have a home that you are trying to pay off the mortgage, you may still find some of the information in this chapter helpful. Plus, who knows when you might want or need to move again.

I want to outline the process of buying a home. Whether you have bought a home or two in the past or you are a first-time home buyer you will find this information helpful.

Path to Homeownership

I want to walk you down the path of Homeownership. My goal is to help you understand the steps involved in the process of buying a home.

Maybe it's been a while since you last bought a home or maybe you are a First Time Home Buyer. Either way I want to give you 15 steps to buying a home.

I have condensed the "Path to Homeownership" down to a convenient downloadable check list, check it out on the **Buying** section of my website REinvestWise.com/Resources.

1. **Find a Good Lender**
   Some people prefer to go to their current bank and if your bank offers home loan products then that would be a good place to start. You may also want to check out other local lenders that specialize in home loan products.

2. **Get Preapproved**
   This step is very important. This will allow you to find out your purchase limit and it will help you know what your closing costs will be. I would also like to point out that almost every property you look at will require you to be preapproved before you can put in an offer.

3. **Decide on a Budget**
   You may not want to go right up to your limit when purchasing a home. You might be approved for $150,000 but you may be more comfortable staying around $125,000.

4. **Find a Good Local Realtor**
   I like to stress the LOCAL part. The Realtor that you decide to work with should be an expert in the local market and should have experience in the area you prefer to move to.

5. **Make a Needs and Wants List**
   Once you make your two separate lists give it to your Realtor, so they can get to work finding you your dream home.

6. **Decide on a Location**
   Unless you are relocating you probably already know where your desired location is. If you are relocating, you will then need to rely on your Realtor to help you find a location that fits your needs.

7. **Research that Location**
   Your Realtor will be able to help you in this area. You will want to know as much as you can about your location including home values and amenities to make sure that area is a good fit for you and your family. This will also help you to be confident that you end up with a good deal on the home you purchase.

8. **Start Your Home Search**
   Finally, we get to the fun part. By now you have nailed down your budget, location and type of home that you desire. Since you have already gone through steps 1-7 your Realtor can narrow your search down to homes you will truly be interested in.

9. **Find Your Dream Home**
   I always tell my buyers that they will know when they have walked into "The ONE" they must have. I remember when I found my own home, we looked for about two months then finally we walked into "The One". We just knew this home was it, we wrote the offer up right then. When you find the right one you will know.

10. **Make an Offer**
    It's very exciting for buyers to put in an offer. You will want to make sure your offer reflects the current market conditions.

11. **Negotiate**
    This is where good Realtors shine! Your Realtor will be able to guide you through the negotiation process. If you put in a good offer to begin with there may not be much to negotiate but I guarantee if you "Low Balled" the offer, then this process will take some time and energy.

12. **Hire a Good Home Inspector**
    Most buyers think that once they have an accepted offer all the work is done, but a whole new set of chores have just begun. You need to schedule all inspections and have all repairs

completed before closing. This may take some more negotiating.

13. Find a Good Home Insurance Provider

This may be easy if you already have a good insurance agent and a policy that you are comfortable with. First Time Home Buyers will have a little more work involved trying to find a good insurance agent and policy and learning everything they need to know to understand their policy.

14. Avoid All Credit Purchases

Making a credit purchase at this point of the process can ruin the whole deal. Never buy anything that involves a loan, like a vehicle. Be very careful when purchasing items with your credit card, make sure you have your balances paid down.

15. Closing and Moving

You made it! The title company will schedule a time for you to sign all the closing documents. I want to point out that in a typical transaction you will not receive keys to your new home at closing. You will have to wait until the title company files the deed at the county recorder's office. This could happen the same day as closing but it is usually the next business day.

The Path to Homeownership may seem complicated but if you are working with a good local Realtor, they will be able to guide you each step of the way.

Understanding the process of buying a home is important. Not only will you have a better home buying process, but you may be able to save hundreds or even thousands of dollars on things like Purchase Price, Repairs, Insurance, Closing Costs and more.

I also want to talk about the fact that the "average" American homeowner moves before the mortgage is paid in full. I have seen reports that say as often as every six years and I have also seen reports that say the average is higher, about twelve to thirteen years.

Why is this important? Every time you buy a home you are paying closing costs and when you are using a mortgage to buy a home you will also be paying piles of money in interest on the mortgage. If your goal is to reach mortgage freedom, which it should be, then you will have a hard time if you move every five or six years.

Your goal should be to find your dream home, or what I like to call it, your "Forever" home and work really hard and be dedicated to paying it off as fast as you can. Once you pay off your home you will have so much more freedom in your life, and you will also have more freedom to move without having to pay all that interest on a new mortgage or lender fees.

If you are already in a home and paying on your mortgage you should have the same goal to pay it off. The benefits of paying off your mortgage quickly are extraordinary whether it is your "Forever" home or you will need to move in the future, or whether you are buying your first home, or you have already been in your home for five years.

Chapter Five

Make Extra Payments

Making extra payments is the key to paying off your mortgage fast! I will go over all the numbers shortly, but I want to make sure you understand what I mean by making extra payments on your mortgage.

There are a few ways you can "make extra payments" on your mortgage and I will go over each of them.

1. Make Extra Payments Yearly

This is a way to send extra payments into your mortgage company on a yearly basis. You can set up a schedule, whether you want to do every six months, quarterly or once a year. You should make sure you add this to your monthly budget!

If you want to make one extra payment a year, then divide up your monthly mortgage payment by twelve and put that money aside. In twelve months, you will have an extra payment ready to send in. You can do this for twice a year payments or quarterly payments, just divide your monthly payment by six or three and put the money aside for the same number of months.

This is not my favorite way of making extra payments because you have money sitting there that you can use to help you pay less interest. Basically, you are losing money every month it sits there.

2. Make Extra Payments Monthly

This, in my opinion, is a way better option. I don't actually mean that you have to make a whole extra payment every month, but you can. My wife and I only made between $40,000 and $65,000 a year together when we were paying off our mortgage and we made double and triple payments every month.

You may not be able to do a double or triple payment every month and that's ok. You can still pay your home off quickly. This monthly method works best if you just simply put extra money on the payment you already send in monthly. Make sure you mark on the payment slip that the extra money is to go towards the **Principal Balance**. You may need to call your mortgage company to ask them how to make sure your extra payment is going towards principal.

With this method you will put every extra dollar you have, after your budget is taken care of, toward your mortgage payment. You need to make every dollar count to be able to pay your mortgage off fast.

This is one of the most effective way of paying your mortgage off fast, I will go over the numbers shortly.

3. Make Bonus Payments

This is an excellent way to put extra money that you receive throughout the year towards paying off your mortgage.

This method will include income sources like Income Tax Returns, Bonuses from work and any side job money you earn. You will take the extra income as it comes to you and put it on your mortgage payment to pay down the principal balance. Large lump sum payments like this will make a huge impact on your mortgage and the interest you pay on the life of the loan.

I suggest using this method in connection with the number two method, "Making extra payments monthly". Using the two methods together will give you the best route to paying off your mortgage fast. You will be able to take years off your mortgage and tens of thousands of dollars of interest will be saved.

I personally used this hybrid method of combining methods number two and three. I was able to pay off my mortgage in just under five years. We had a mortgage of about $72,000 and we payed it off in less then five years making on average $55,000 per year.

You can do it too!

4. Make Bi-weekly Payments

This is not the method I used but it can be helpful when trying to pay your mortgage off early. This is a good method if you are not able to put much extra on the monthly payments or if you are not very good at saving money.

People that tend to spend their money as fast as they get it will have a hard time paying off their mortgage quickly unless they put themselves into a structured payment plan like bi-weekly payments. This will force you or allow you (depending on how you look at it), to pay **26 Half payments** each year instead of the normal **12 Whole payments** in a year.

This plan equals out to one extra whole payment each year and it will take years off your mortgage and save you thousands of dollars in interest during the length of the loan.

If you go with the bi-weekly payments method, you can either have your loan set up with bi-weekly payments or you can just simply pay a half payment every two weeks. Check with your mortgage company to help you determine what option is best for you.

How Much Can You Save Making Extra Payments?

Now I am going to go over the numbers and show you exactly how much money you will save by making extra payments and paying off your mortgage early.

I always tell my buyers and any homeowner I meet that you should put something extra on every mortgage payment even if it is only $5. It adds up and it will save you money!

For our examples we are going to use a mortgage loan amount of $200,000 and we are going to assume the home was just purchased and we are on mortgage payment number one of a thirty-year mortgage. Your situation will probably be different then this so you should utilize a mortgage calculator to figure out your specific payoff plan.

Use my Mortgage Calculators on my website. **REinvestWise.com/homeowner**

Making Extra Payments Yearly

This will be making one extra payment per year, two extra payments per year and making one extra payment quarterly (or four extra payments per year) and starting on the first year of the loan.

Loan payments on this loan are assumed to be **$1,557**, so you would be paying additional $1,557 payments.

Extra Payments Per Year	0	1	2	4
Total Interest Paid	$186,512	$139,673	$112,162	$80,586
Years Until payoff	30	23.5	19.5	14.5
Total Paid for Home	$386,512	$339,673	$312,162	$280,586
Total Money Saved	$0	$46,839	$74,350	$105,926
Years Paid Off Early	0	6.5	10.5	15.5

As you can see making even just one extra payment per year will make a huge difference!

Making Extra Payments Monthly

This is where you will be putting extra money on each payment every month.

Extra Payment Per Month	$25	$100	$250	$500
Total Interest Paid	$175,444	$149,443	$116,141	$85,390
Years Until payoff	28.5	25	20	15
Total Paid for Home	$375,444	$349,443	$316,141	$285,390
Total Money Saved	$11,068	$37,069	$70,371	$101,122
Years Paid Off Early	1.5	5	10	15

As you can see if all you did was add an extra $25 a month onto your mortgage payment you would save $11,068 in interest. Everyone can spare an extra $25 a month, if you don't already have it in your budget you can simply not eat out one time a month and you will have the $25 just like that.

REinvestWise.com

Making Bonus Payments Yearly

This is where you put a lump some of money on the mortgage on a yearly basis. This could be a Christmas bonus at work or Income Tax Return, etc.

Extra Payment Per Year	$1,500	$2,000	$4,000	$6,000
Total Interest Paid	$140,949	$130,529	$100,921	$82,302
Years Until payoff	23.5	22	18	15
Total Paid for Home	$340,949	$330,529	$300,921	$282,302
Total Money Saved	$45,563	$55,983	$85,591	$104,210
Years Paid Off Early	6.5	8	12	15

If you utilize this method, you can keep your monthly budget the same and just put the extra money you receive throughout the year onto the principal balance of your mortgage.

Making Bi-weekly Payments

Now we will look at just simply going to bi-weekly payments instead of regular monthly payments.

	Monthly Payments	Bi-weekly Payments
Total Interest Paid	$186,512	$139,673
Years Until payoff	30	23.5
Total Paid for Home	$386,512	$339,673
Total Money Saved	$0	$46,839
Years Paid Off Early	0	6.5

This method is essentially making one extra payment a year. I only suggest this method if you don't think you will be disciplined enough to make extra payments on your own. If making extra payments or putting extra money towards your principal every month won't be an issue for you then I suggest that you use one of the other methods.

Should You Go With a 15 Year Mortgage Instead of a 30 Year Mortgage?

This is a very good question. There are a few advantages of a 15-year mortgage over a 30-year mortgage but not everyone will be able to qualify for a 15-year mortgage especially if it is their first home.

Most home buyers will not qualify for a 15-year loan for the amount they need to buy the home that they need. Therefore, most home buyers go with a 30-year loan. The reason most home buyers cannot qualify for the 15-year loan is because of the income requirements. The monthly mortgage payment will be between 30-40% higher than the traditional 30-year mortgage.

If you can qualify for the 15-year mortgage, then you should by all means go with a 15-year mortgage. You should get a lower interest rate and therefore you will pay less interest. You can and should still put extra money on your mortgage payments when going with a 15-year mortgage, but you may not be able to put quite as much as you could if you went with a 30-year mortgage.

How Can You Pay Off Your Mortgage in Under 5 Years?

As I mentioned before, I paid off my mortgage in under five years. I am going to be honest with you, this will not be easy! There are a few key factors that made a huge difference in allowing me to pay my mortgage off in under five years.

1. Don't Over Buy

This is extremely important! When we started looking for a home, the first thing we did was get pre-approved for a home loan. The bank we went to gave us a pre-approval of $100,000. We started looking for homes around $50,000. We couldn't find anything that suited our needs and we did not want to buy a "Starter" house and then move again, we wanted our "Forever" home!

We then decided to raise our search budget to $80,000 and about the same time our dream home fell into that range. We made a good offer, they accepted, we put some money down and our mortgage was for about $72,000.

Notice we could have gone up to $100,000 but we didn't. We stayed as low as we could with still getting the home we needed and wanted. The lower loan amount played a key role in allowing us to be able to pay our mortgage off so quickly.

2. Don't Over Spend

This is where your budget will play a key role in your ability to pay your mortgage off fast. You need to save every dollar you can every day to be able to pay your mortgage off in under five years.

Now we still ate out and, in my opinion, we ate out too much, but we didn't eat out every day and most of the times that we dined out we would share a meal or order from a value menu. We did everything we could to be able to save money even when we were "treating" ourselves with a nice meal out.

It is not just food that will "eat" away at your budget. Entertainment can add up quite fast. Going to the movies can cost a small fortune for a family of four or five.

One thing that some people struggle with is buying a pop or candy bar at the check out or gas station. This was never a problem for me because I would see the price for that 20oz pop and think I could get a whole 2-liter for that same price.

All of these things add up, every dollar you don't spend on these items is one more dollar you can put on your mortgage.

3. Make More Money

This will mean different things to different people. Some people will have an opportunity to get a new job or promotion while others may have the opportunity to work overtime. Another option would be to get a side "Hustle" to make some extra cash.

We did all these things. We got new jobs that paid better, I took a promotion, we worked as much overtime as they would give us, and I did some side jobs to make extra money.

When we bought our home, we were making about $40,000 a year and by the time we paid it off we were making $65,000 a year. It took hard work and dedication. We were both working 50-60 hours a week, but I will be honest the excitement of the mortgage getting lower ever month made it tolerable.

You may not need to work 60 hours a week, but you should try to work a little overtime. You may be able to ask for a raise or a promotion and increase your income substantially.

There are always ways to make extra money. You need to find something you can do on the side or a part time job to add to your income. This is essential to being able to pay off your mortgage in under five years.

4. Put Every Dollar on Your Mortgage

This is probably obvious to you by now. We did this every month. We would pay all our bills then look to see what we have left, and we would put everything we could on the principal balance of our mortgage. We did not drain our account to zero, would leave some emergency money in the account.

You need to make sure you build up your savings and emergency fund before you start putting all your money on your mortgage. Once you get your money in savings all set, you need to start putting every dollar on your mortgage.

If you have other loans and debts, you may need to take care of these first and it may make the five-year mark unreachable, but you can still work hard and pay off your mortgage fast. My wife and I did not have any other debts when we bought our home, our mortgage was the only thing we had a loan for. This put us in the perfect position to pay off our mortgage in under five years.

Chapter Six

You Can Be Mortgage Free

You can reach your goal of being mortgage free. No matter what your situation is you can pay off your mortgage before the thirty-year term. It will take some planning, dedication and hard work but you can do it.

You don't have to be rich to be able to pay off your mortgage early. Anyone can do it! No matter what your income level is you can do things to set your self up to become mortgage free!

What if you have huge debt?

If you feel overwhelmed and you feel like you are drowning in debt, don't worry, you can do this! If you have substantial debt that should be your first and primary focus. Once you get your debts paid off you can work on paying off your mortgage.

When it comes to paying off your debts, the best and fastest way to do this is to use the "Snowball" method. First, make sure you pay all of your bills every month, at least pay the minimum amount due. Then take the debt with the smallest balance and put everything you have on it until its paid off. Then you move to the next biggest balance and put everything you have on that bill. After you pay each debt off you will find that you will be able to pay more towards the next debt. By the time you get to the largest debt you will have a substantial amount of money to pay it down quicker.

You will find that once you get one or two payed off you will start to get really excited about putting all the extra money on the next one and getting that paid off as well. It will become a way of life for you, almost like you are addicted to paying off your debts.

I personally know a husband and wife that was able to pay off ten credit cards (with a total of well over $10,000) in just over one year. You can do it too!

When you eventually get all your debts paid off you will then be able to throw all that money at your mortgage and knock that out too.

You Can Do This!

Whether you have huge debts or not you can pay your mortgage off much faster than the 30-year term they want you to have. The longer it takes you to pay off your mortgage the more money the lender will make in interest, so the faster you pay your mortgage off the more money you will save!

You have nothing to lose from paying off your mortgage early! You will only gain from it. If you pay your taxes and home owners insurance in escrow through your mortgage company, you will have to save monthly for this expense to be paid every six months. Other then that small adjustment to your budget there is nothing left to do but start building up your savings accounts.

You can live like a king after you pay off your mortgage, but I wouldn't suggest that. Yes, you should put a little more in the budget for "fun" things like entertainment, food, vacations but try not to go too crazy.

I am big fan of real estate investing and I would suggest you put your money toward that AFTER you pay your mortgage off. If you think you would be interested in real estate investing, but you don't have any experience, I would suggest you check out my book **"ANYONE Can Invest In Real Estate"**.

Of course, Real Estate Investing isn't your only option, you can invest in anything or you could start a business, or you can simply just build up your savings. You can use this as a goal to help encourage yourself to pay off your mortgage quickly.

You can do this, you can pay off your debts and your mortgage, once you set out to do it, even if you have setbacks just remember to **Keep Moving Forward!**

www.ingramcontent.com/pod-product-compliance
Lightning Source LLC
Chambersburg PA
CBHW021507210526
45463CB00002B/938